This book belongs to:

Dedicated to
**Max and his amazing
Grand Pa Duncan**

A TEMPLAR BOOK

First published in the UK in 2026 by Templar Books,
an imprint of Bonnier Books UK
5th Floor, HYLO, 105 Bunhill Row,
London, EC1Y 8LZ

The authorised representative in the EEA is
Bonnier Books UK (Ireland) Limited.
Registered office address: Block B, The Crescent Building,
Northwood, Santry, Dublin 9, D09 C6X8, Ireland
compliance@bonnierbooks.ie
www.bonnierbooks.co.uk

Text copyright © 2026 by Templar Books
Illustration copyright © 2026 by Seb Braun
Design copyright © 2026 by Templar Books

10 9 8 7 6 5 4 3 2 1

All rights reserved

ISBN 978-1-80078-576-2

This book was typeset in Mr Dodo and MixModern
The illustrations were created digitally

Written by Ruth Symons
Edited by Victoria Garrard
Designed by Lorraine Monagle
Production by Nick Read
Consultant: Lizzie Noble,
Certified Forest Childcare Provider

Printed in China

Stay safe!
It's important to stay
safe while you play outside.
This symbol will warn you when
you need to take extra care.

Forest School kit list:

Water bottle

Waterproofs

Something to eat

Sturdy shoes

Extras for a sunny day:

Sun cream

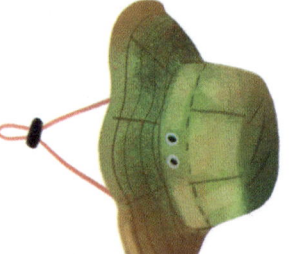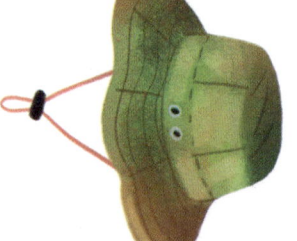
Sun hat

Long-sleeved top

Deep in the woods, beneath the trees, the animals are gathering. It's time for Mrs Owl's Forest School!

Mouse, Squirrel, Fox and Rabbit sit in a circle. It's a sunny day, and the light falls in dappled shapes around their feet.

Mouse, Squirrel, Fox and Rabbit are in a shady spot, even though it is sunny. What is the light like where you are? Can you see any shadows?

"Today, we're going on a treasure hunt!" says Mrs Owl.

"What's that?" asks Fox.

"It's a special kind of game. I've left a trail of clues for you all to follow. Each clue leads to the next one. And at the end, you'll find some... treasure!"

MRS OWL'S GUIDE TO TRAIL-MAKING

Remember to leave marks in ways that won't harm nature and can be easily removed when you're finished playing.

Using sticks, chalk or drawing in the mud are all good techniques.

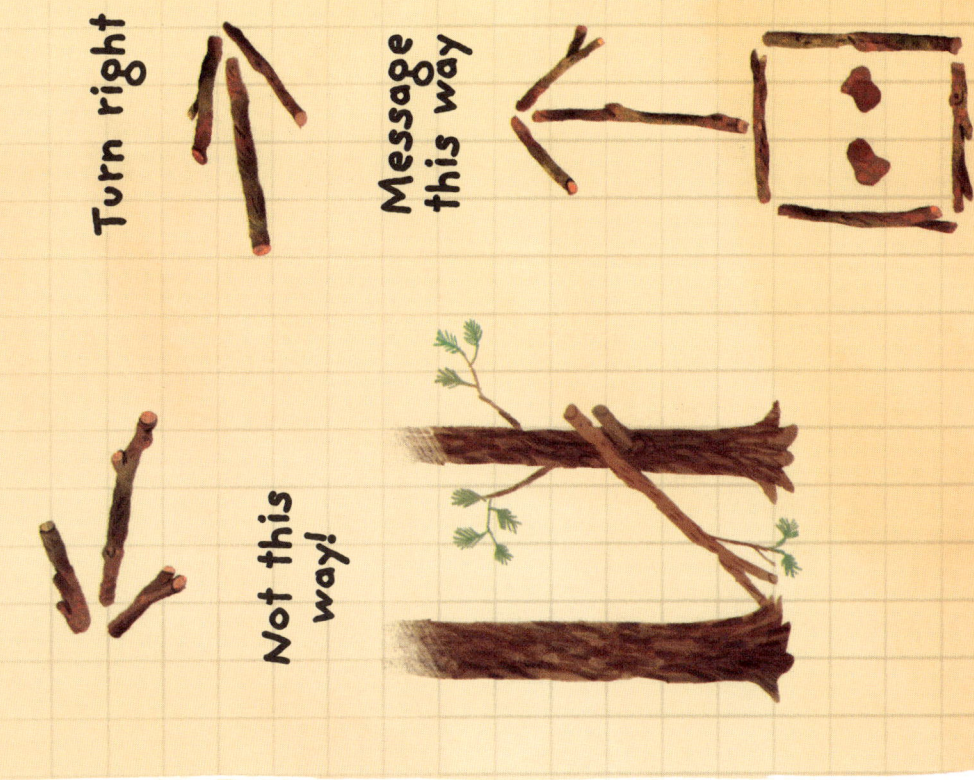

Turn left

Turn right

Message this way

Not this way!

"But what do the clues look like?" asks Squirrel.

"They can look like marks or symbols. Today, we're using special signs made from sticks," says Mrs Owl.

"And if you ever get stuck, remember this: look up, look down, look all around. Now off we go!"

"I see one too," says Squirrel. "It's pointing right."

"I see one," says Mouse. "It's pointing straight ahead."

The friends look carefully around them.

"I see one as well," says Fox. "It's pointing left."

"Remember," says Mrs Owl, "look up, look down, look all around."
"I can't see any," says Rabbit.

This sign is on the big tree!
"I see it!" says Rabbit.

The friends are getting very good at spotting clues. And Rabbit's been spotting some other things, too.

"I'm not just finding clues," says Rabbit. "I can see an acorn and a stick and a dandelion. Can I pick it?"

MRS OWL'S GUIDE TO FLOWERS

Can you spot any of these flowers on your next walk?

- Forget-me-not
- Dandelion
- Daisy
- Foxglove
- Poppy
- Cornflower

"It's best to leave wild flowers for the insects," says Mrs Owl.

"But you can pick up the acorns if you like."

Take care around wild flowers, as some are poisonous, even to touch! It's best to admire or draw them but not touch them.

The little Forest School friends have come a very long way now.

"This sign is strange," says Squirrel. "What does it mean?"

"It means that if you go this way, you'll find a special message."

They creep forwards, looking carefully at the bushes, trees and grass all around them for clues.

Maybe they've nearly found the treasure!

"There!" says Fox, pointing excitedly. "It's a..."

"...TREASURE MAP!"

They all gather quickly around the treasure map.

"Wow!" says Mouse. "And look – X marks the spot. That's where the treasure will be!"

...under the very tall tree...

...through the field of swaying flowers...

They follow the map...

...around the big rock...

...through the gate...

...and over the bridge.

"We've had an adventure," says Fox.

"Fox is right," laughs Mrs Owl. "When you're having fun, even a walk in the woods can become an adventure!"

"But wait – this is where the treasure should be," says Squirrel. "This is where we started. We haven't been anywhere!"

"Yes, we have!" says Mouse. "We've walked for MILES!"

"And look," says Squirrel pointing. "X marks the spot!"

"But where's the treasure? It's just a piece of paper," says Rabbit. "What does it say?" asks Fox.

Mrs Owl reads it aloud:

If you want a shiny treat, look in the place where you put your feet!

"But I'm wearing my shoes," says Squirrel. Everyone looks a bit confused.

"What about the wet-weather wellies?" Mouse rushes over to check.

Each animal has a bag of gold chocolate coins in their boots.

"Wow, shiny treasure!" says Fox. Everyone is so excited.

How do surprises make you feel? Do they make you excited or make you feel worried? Can you think of a time when you were surprised?

But Rabbit has her hands full. "I found other treasure," she says. "Look at ALL these acorns I gathered."

Rabbit has picked up heaps and heaps of acorns.

"You're right," says Mrs Owl. "Treasure comes in many forms, and nature is full of treasures. What are you going to do with all those acorns?"

"I could put them in a pirate treasure chest?" suggests Rabbit.

"Yes, you could," says Mrs Owl. "Or you could plant them if you like? One day they might turn into a huge tree like the one we saw today!"

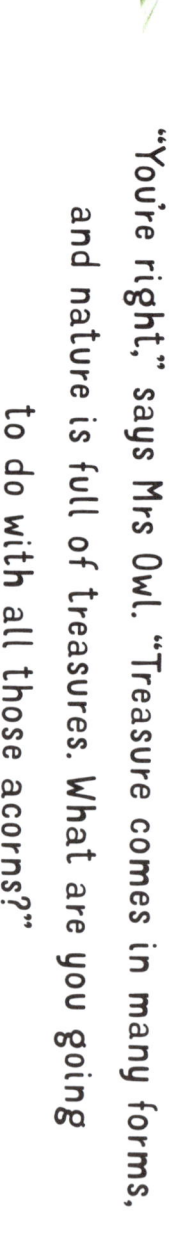

MRS OWL'S GUIDE TO PLANTING ACORNS

You will need:

Acorns

A bucket

Plant pot or old yoghurt pot

Compost

1. The best acorns to plant are ones that have recently fallen. Look for ones that are mostly brown and aren't damaged.

2. Put the acorns in a bucket of water – leave out any that float.

3. Make a hole in the compost and place your acorn in it. Gently cover with more compost.

4. Don't forget to water your pot.

5. When the seedling gets bigger, you can move the plant into a bigger pot.

"Good work," says Mrs Owl. "Now, who's thirsty?"

Every day at Mrs Owl's Forest School ends the same way. The animals sit around the campfire, sipping their toasty hot drinks.

Fires can be dangerous! Only light a fire with a supervising adult. Never leave it unattended, and don't get too close.

The sun is going down and it's getting a little chilly. What a lovely but tiring day!

"It's home time now," says Mrs Owl. "See you next time you come to Forest School."

Everyone can enjoy what Forest School has to offer. It doesn't matter if you go to Forest School or if you've never heard of it! Whether you live in the countryside or the city, you can try some of these activities...

SCAVENGER HUNT

Why don't you go on a scavenger hunt instead of a treasure hunt? Make a list of things to look for and tick them off as you go for a walk in the countryside, the park or your garden.

Try looking for:

- ☐ A green leaf
- ☐ A feather
- ☐ A brown leaf
- ☐ A bug
- ☐ A smooth rock
- ☐ A flower

Hi!

JOURNEY STICK

You could make a 'journey stick' and gather things as you go – just like Rabbit!

Cut a strip of cardboard and put a piece of double-sided tape down one side. Peel off the backing so it's really sticky. Then stick on things you find along your way, like feathers, fallen leaves or seeds.

MAKE A TREASURE MAP

Try drawing a map of your local park, garden or even sitting room! Can you plot a route around it and give it to a friend? Don't forget to leave a special treat where the X is on the map!

Never go anywhere without a responsible adult. If you go into the woods, make sure an adult has a fully charged phone with them in case of emergency.

Why not tell a scavenger story using all the things you found on your hunt? Or tell the story of your own hunt, just like the story in this book!

Join

Mrs Owl's FOREST·SCHOOL

for another adventure in:

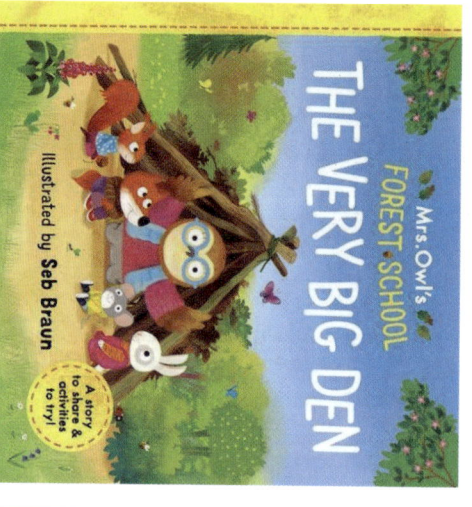
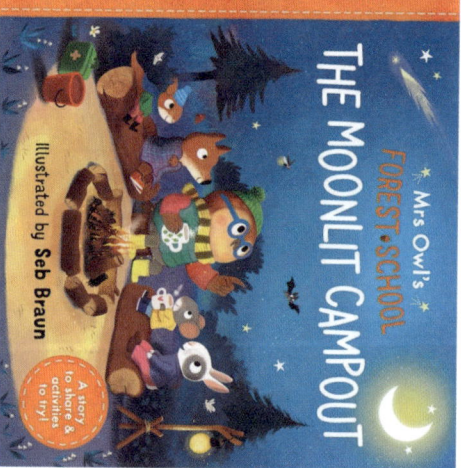
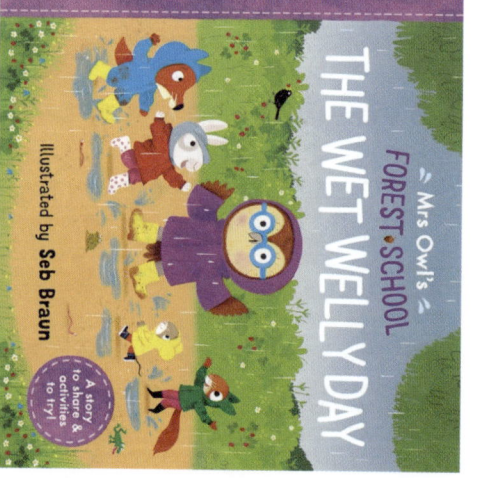